Greek Myths
THE WOODEN HORSE

JILL DUDLEY

PUT IT IN YOUR POCKET SERIES
ORPINGTON PUBLISHERS

Published by
Orpington Publishers

Cover design and origination by
Creeds, Bridport, Dorset
01308 423411

Printed and bound in the UK by
Creeds

© Jill Dudley 2016

ISBN: 978-0-9934890-2-0

THE WOODEN HORSE

The Wooden Horse, otherwise known as the Trojan Horse, was an extraordinary and imaginative plot devised by the Greek warrior Odysseus.* It was this which was finally to bring about the end of the ten-year Trojan War.

The war was fought by the Greeks as a matter of honour. The beautiful Helen,* wife of Menelaus, king of Sparta, had run off with Paris, the handsome son of King Priam of Troy. Paris had been sent as an envoy to Sparta where he had been welcomed as an honoured guest. When the king was called away to attend to the funeral of his grandfather in Crete, Paris seduced Helen and persuaded her to abandon her husband and young daughter, and return with him to Troy. This gross abuse of the king's hospitality was a disgraceful breach of etiquette. Worse still Paris took with him not only his host's wife, but a quantity of Spartan treasure too.

In young Paris' defence this love affair was not entirely his fault. Their passion was the work of Aphrodite, goddess of love. In the contest known as The Judgement of Paris,* it was she who had promised Paris the most beautiful woman in the world if he chose her as 'the fairest'. The contest had taken place on Mt. Ida between Aphrodite and two other goddesses Hera and Athena who, in contrast to Aphrodite's bribe, offered him somewhat boring things such as power and victory respectively.

In the tenth year of the war Odysseus, often referred to by Homer as 'resourceful' or 'cunning', realized that Troy would never fall unless Trojan morale could be undermined. To do this he knew he had to steal the *palladium* from the temple of Athena in the city. The *palladium* was a wooden statue of the goddess, believed to have fallen from heaven in answer to the prayers of Ilus, the founder of Troy. Its presence in the city assured its safety, or so the Trojans liked to believe.

Both warring factions worshipped the goddess Athena but, because she had not been chosen as 'the fairest' at the Judgement, Athena gave her support to the Greeks, and turned a deaf ear to the prayers of the Trojans, unlike Apollo who never wavered from helping them.

On the night of the planned theft Odysseus and the warrior Diomedes disguised themselves as beggars and, under cover of darkness, entered the city. It is said that as they made their way to the temple they came across Helen who recognized them but, instead of handing them over to the Trojans, helped them steal the sacred talisman. By this late stage of the war, Helen's beloved Paris had been killed, and she had married his brother Deiphobus. It is believed that by now she was full of remorse at the number of men who had died in battle because of her. Secretly she wanted to return home to Sparta, to her husband and their daughter Hermione.

With the *palladium* in the Greek camp, 'resourceful' Odysseus now thought up the ploy which was to bring about the final destruction of the city. He instructed the master craftsman Epeios to build a gigantic Wooden Horse, large enough to conceal inside it thirty (some say forty) of the most courageous heroes of the Greek army. This Wooden Horse with its band of hand-picked warriors was left on the Trojan plain in full view of the city.

The Greek army next set fire to their huts in Beşik bay where they had camped throughout the war, and set sail as though for home. Instead, the fleet dropped anchor behind the nearby island of Tenedos. The stratagem worked. Believing that the war was over after ten years of anguish, the Trojans threw open their gates and celebrated with great joy, pouring down from their city to the Trojan plain to examine the huge Trojan Horse,

In the course of their euphoria some shepherds came across a hapless Greek who had been left behind. He was in shackles, and they quickly brought him to King Priam who was amongst his people celebrating. The Greek captive was Sinon and was, in fact, part of the Greek plot. He acted the part of the terrified prisoner who had managed to escape from becoming a sacrificial victim to Athena. For some time, Sinon pointed out, there had been violent storms and, to ensure a safe passage home, his people had questioned Apollo's oracle and had been told their journey home could only be achieved if one of them was offered up as a human sacrifice. Sinon claimed that Odysseus had taken a dislike to him, so the choice of sacrificial victim had fallen on him. With tears, and assurances that he was speaking the truth, he told them how he had miraculously managed to escape, and had been hiding in the reeds fearing capture. Keeping up his convincing performance of the terrified escapee, he threw himself on their mercy, and the kindly King Priam believed him, and ordered that he should be freed from his bonds and cared for.

When asked about the Wooden Horse, Sinon explained that it had been left there as a gift for the goddess Athena in an endeavour to appease her for the sacrilege of stealing her *palladium*. He described how some of his people had seen fire flashing from the image's eyes, and how it sometimes appeared to lunge aggressively towards those who looked at it, striking fear into them.

Sinon's explanation sounded so plausible and convincing – the Trojans were renowned horse breeders to whom horses were sacred – that King Priam was persuaded that the Horse should immediately be brought into their city and placed before Athena's temple to show gratitude to the goddess for their unexpected victory.

Though the majority went along with Sinon's story, there were a few who remained suspicious, notably Laocoon, a priest of Poseidon. Laocoon did his best to dissuade the Trojans from accepting this so-called gift to Athena. It would mean making a breach in the defence walls to get it inside, and he warned them against it. He went as far as plunging his spear into the Horse's flank where it remained quivering on impact; it was fortunate that none of the Greek warriors inside was hurt, and none shouted out.

The priest had no sooner stabbed this so-called offering to the goddess when a horrific event occurred which could only be regarded by the Trojans as divine retribution for their suspicious rejection of this Greek gift to their goddess. Two huge serpents appeared from the nearby island of Tenedos behind which the Greek fleet was hidden. The first century B.C. writer Virgil in his *Aeneid* described the serpents as witnessed by his Trojan hero Aeneas: *'...their fore-parts and their blood-red crests towered above the waves; the rest drove through the ocean behind, wreathing monstrous coils, and leaving a wake that roared and foamed. And now, with blazing and blood-shot eyes and tongues which flickered and licked their hissing mouths, they were on the beach...'* (Aeneid 2:207-212) In an instant each had devoured the priest's two small sons before seizing Laocoon *'...in the giant spirals of their scaly length, twice round his middle, twice round his throat...His hands strove frantically to wrench the knots apart...His shrieks were horrible...'* (Aeneid 2:217-221) With Laocoon and his two sons dead, the two serpents went on up to the citadel and into Athena's temple where they vanished behind the shield carried by her cult statue.

This fearful and sinister occurrence filled the Trojans with terror. They needed no more convincing that the Wooden Horse must immediately be moved from the Trojan plain up to their citadel and placed as an offering before the temple of the goddess.

King Priam's daughter Cassandra was another to cry out her forebodings. But all was in vain. Cassandra had once been the object of Apollo's affections, but had rejected him, and Apollo in his anger had bestowed on her the gift of prophecy with the unfortunate curse that nobody would ever believe her. So it was that, despite her warnings, she was ignored. A portion of the defence walls of the city, therefore, was dismantled to allow the Wooden Horse to be dragged inside and brought to the temple.

Once inside it is said that the beautiful Helen with her new husband Deiphobus came to see this wonder. Either she had changed her mind about returning to Sparta, or felt snubbed that the Greek army had sailed without her, or even because she suspected a ruse, she now circled around the towering Wooden Horse, calling out the names of the warriors and mimicking the voices of their wives to entice them out. It had taken all Odysseus' persuasive powers to prevent his companions, one of whom was her former husband King Menelaus of Sparta, from answering her.

Later that night the Greek fleet set sail from their hiding place behind Tenedos. They had timed it well because it was a dark and moonless night. Within the city Sinon was on the watch for their pre-arranged fire-signal which would alert him that the fleet was on the move. Seeing it, Sinon was at last able to draw back the wooden bars on the horse which released the warriors. Together with the newly arrived reinforcements, they went on the rampage, ransacking, killing and setting fire to the city.

King Menelaus, the hapless cuckolded husband of the beautiful Helen, whilst ransacking the city came across her cowering in the house of her new husband Deiphobus. He raised his sword intending to kill her, but Aphrodite intervened. It is said that Helen lowered her garment and bared her breast to him, and all his anger melted away. Far from killing her, his sword dropped from his hand and he felt nothing but overwhelming love. Nothing is certain, but later writers reported that together they sailed to Egypt where, due to the displeasure of the gods, they remained until Menelaus managed to appease the deities, after which he and his queen sailed back to Greece and returned to their royal duties at Sparta.

His brother, King Agamemnon of Mycenae, returned home bringing Cassandra as his concubine. It was a tragic irony that after ten years of facing death on the battlefield, he came home to his palace only to be murdered by his wife. His story became the subject of the great tragic dramatist Aeschylus' trilogy *The Oresteia*.

What happened to the Trojan Horse? Well, its fate is unknown but, no doubt, its pinewood structure went up in flames together with the city. However, its story has never been forgotten. Down the millennia it has been the subject for writers, historians and poets; it has been depicted by artists on *amphorae;* it has been a subject for debate by scholars. Some dismiss the story outright and say it was some sort of siege machine, and the heroes hiding in it pure fallacy. The truth about it will probably never be known, but what does it matter? The story of the Wooden Horse has been told and retold down the centuries and, although over three thousand years have passed, it is still remembered.

* Denotes a separate booklet on the subject.

GLOSSARY OF GODS AND HEROES

APHRODITE – The goddess of love. She backed the Trojans in the war.

APOLLO – Son of Zeus and Leto. He was god of music, archery and prophecy. He sided with the Trojans in the war.

ATHENA – Daughter of Zeus. She was born mature and fully armed from his head. She was goddess of handicraft, and protectress of many cities, but especialy Athens. She was the embodiment of wisdom, and in the Trojan War she supported the Greeks.

CASSANDRA – Daughter of King Priam of Troy and Hecuba. She had the gift of prophecy but nobody believed her.

DEIPHOBUS – Son of King Priam and Hecuba. After Paris was killed he married Helen.

DIOMEDES – A Greek hero and close companion of Odysseus.

HELEN – Daughter of Tyndareus, king of Sparta, and Leda. It is believed Zeus loved Leda and turned himself into a swan to seduce her, and Helen was really his daughter.

HERA – Wife of Zeus. She was goddess of women and marriage, and supported the Greeks in the Trojan War.

HERMIONE – Daughter of Helen and Menelaus.

LAOCOON – A priest of Poseidon. Laocoon advised the Trojans not to bring the Wooden Horse into their city, for which he and his two sons were strangled by two huge serpents from the sea.

MENELAUS – King of Sparta and husband of Helen.

ODYSSEUS – Son of Laertes, king of Ithaka. A great Greek warrior.

PARIS – Son of King Priam of Troy and his wife Hecuba. He seduced Menelaus' wife Helen and ran off with her, hence the Trojan War to get her back.

PRIAM – King of Troy, husband of Hecuba, and father of Paris.

POSEIDON – God of the sea, earthquakes and horses. He supported the Greeks in tne Trojan War.

SINON – An unsung Greek hero and spy. He pretended he had escaped from being offered up as a human sacrifice, and the Trojans took him in to their city which led to their final downfall.

ZEUS – Supreme god of the ancient world, and husband of Hera.

ACKNOWLEDGEMENT

Grateful acknowledgement to W. F. Knight's translation of Virgil's *The Aeneid*, Penguin Books Ltd. edition, published 1956.

MORE FROM THE
PUT IT IN YOUR POCKET SERIES

GREEK ISLAND MYTHS

ALL YOU NEED TO KNOW ABOUT
THE ISLAND'S MYTHS, LEGENDS
AND ITS GODS

CHIOS

CRETE

KOS

NAXOS

RHODES

SANTORINI

ALSO BY JILL DUDLEY

YE GODS! (TRAVELS IN GREECE)

YE GODS! II (MORE TRAVELS IN GREECE)

LAP OF THE GODS (TRAVELS IN CRETE
AND THE AEGEAN ISLANDS)